AF208189

HOUSE IT START

an INVESTING GUIDE
to REAL ESTATE

ADAM THORNTON

House It Start

An Investing Guide to Real Estate

Adam Thornton

ISBN (Print Edition): 978-1-66787-713-6

ISBN (eBook Edition): 978-1-66787-714-3

CONTENTS

CORPORATE EMPLOYEE TO FREE AGENCY

INTRODUCTION

L iving in a "Free Country" is always a dream of everyone that comes to America. This is something most Americans take for granted. We grow up learning our ABC's and being taught how to be a "good" employee, but so many of us never get out of the rat race and become truly free. There are many different versions of "free", but this book talks about finding the freedom to do what you want, when you want to do it, through Real Estate. Real Estate is the way I have found that will help the most people become free. This book will touch on ways that Julie, my wife, and I have become financially free, but there are more ways than just what I touch on. I will try to hit them all in one way or another, but the ones I have personally done, I will expand upon further. It is up to you to learn your path to freedom and grow your portfolio. But first, let's start with how it all started for us.

I had the American dream. A corporate America position running operations for a company of 150 employees to manage. In 2017, I was let go of my position and knew I wanted to get into Real Estate. Not knowing where to start, I got my Real Estate License in the state of Ohio. I started with a fast growing brokerage. In Ohio, you have to be under a real estate brokerage in order to have your license; although, the brokerage does not have to be a part of the National Association of Realtors. I quickly went from 0 listings and 0 closings to having over 35 listings with 15 closings within 9 months. I was on fire.

During this time of starting, I knew the market was not going to stay as strong as it was currently going, so I asked questions. I asked our top agent, "What did you do in 2008 during the crash? What allowed you to stay afloat while so many other agents sank and had to get second and third jobs?"

His answer was simple, "Buy Rentals." But how? How do you just say, "Buy rentals?" How do you go from making $44,000 in your first year and taking care of your family of 4 to paying $75,000 for rentals and still being able to take care of your family of 4? I didn't understand. A few months later I was approached to take on a role as an office owner for a very large brokerage. After deliberating about it with my wife, I wondered how to approach my current brokerage I was a part of. I went for it. I asked them to give me an office, which I would pay for out of my pocket, and stay with the company. As I was speaking with the broker, I could tell something wasn't right. Instead of giving the go-ahead of a new office, I got my license turned into the state. Having your license turned in basically means "You're Fired." Ouch. So I moved to the new brokerage. My 35 listings now went to 0 because in Ohio, the broker carries the listing and the agent gets his/her name put on the sign, but the listing belongs to the broker.

Starting over is never fun, but sometimes it's during these times you have to evaluate where you are in life. What could I have done differently? What would I have said differently?

Now, I'm with a great brokerage with more training, but I have nothing to make money. Back to the grind. Back to the door-knocking, handing out flyer after flyer, talking to everyone I meet about real estate. I was back at it, but this time it was different. This time it was to prove my former broker wrong. I had the wrong motive for working hard. I was no longer working for my family but to beat my previous broker. Still this time, I had no money to help me beat my previous broker. It was difficult. But let's go back to where it really started…

2011- Adam meets Julie. Adam and Julie get married. Life is moving fast.

2012-2014- Adam and Julie buy a foreclosed home. We will break down the first deal at the end of the book, but let's just move forward. Next, our son is born. Things change when you have kids. Things that were ok when it was just the two of us we no longer wanted. The pool was a liability. Walking from the garage to the house had issues. The 2 flights of stairs made midnight feedings hard. One time, I even fell down the stairs with my six month old son. I sacrificed my body to keep him safe, so he was okay. Unfortunately, I was stuck on the couch for several days during recovery, which meant I could not help Julie out. The last event that sealed the deal was the waterfall. Let's just say coming home to a waterfall over your television because of the boiler system, is not a good way to end the day. After the repairs were made and bills were paid, we were ready to move. However, we were not ready to give up on our real estate adventures.

2014-2016- First flip and rental

2016- Form Birchwood Homes and Downsize to jump start business

2017-2018- Buy more rentals

2019- Covid hits, rentals cover all bills, plan is working.

2020- Business is booming

2022- Business doubles

STARTING

We all start from nothing. We all start with no properties to our names, unless you were gifted one as a child. We all start from the bottom and work our way up, again, unless you were gifted something from someone along the way. Whether that be at a job, in our careers, starting your business, or buying real estate. It's the decisions we make along the way that get us to the next phases in life and grow ourselves and our family.

We are going to take a high level overview of various real estate options you can consider as you start out. As you figure out what direction you want to pursue, you can search and find more things about each topic we discuss, or I can write my next books diving deeper, whichever is faster for you... My goal for this book is to not go so far in depth that this book is 300 pages. My goal is to get you making the best decision for you and your family and to be able to start doing that right away. End of the day, just start. So many people talk about it, but never start.

CHAPTER 1

DECISIONS, DECISIONS, DECISIONS

DECISIONS, DECISIONS, DECISIONS...

You have decisions to make when starting your real estate journey. No one can make those decisions for you, but this book will help guide you to find what decisions make the most sense to you. Do you start with a Flip? Rental? Wholesaling? BRRRR? Let's take a look at each of these.

FLIPPING

Flipping a home is when you buy a property, rehab (renovate) the property, and sell it for a profit. I started out flipping properties. As I wanted to get started shortly after switching brokerages, I needed capital to start flipping. I didn't have clients banging down my door to buy or sell a house, so I needed to create my own source of income. Flipping made sense. I loved carpentry, which I learned in high school at our local trade school. Mr. Zimmer, my carpentry teacher, was the best teacher. I would not be where I am without his guidance in construction.

My only problem was I didn't have money. Speaking about this problem with a friend of mine at church, he said, "I have the money, but don't have the time." BINGO. He has the cash, I need the cash. I know the skills and have the resources to get inexpensive deals and have the time, he doesn't have the time. It was totally a God thing. Let's say his name is "Ryan." Ryan worked at a corporate position in a wonderful company. He traveled a ton for work but just didn't have the time to get into real estate. Ryan had enough money to get us both started on this journey. Our first house was a flip. We bought the home at a sheriff's auction. Don't worry, we will talk more about this later. We bought it for $34,600, but we knew it was going to take time to get the deed and get renovations completed.

At the time I was working with a buyer for 6 months and was trying to find him the right property for him and his daughter. Let's say his name is "Matt." I told Matt to drive by the property, but that I wouldn't have the deed for a few weeks. We still needed to renovate the property. A few hours later Matt called me and asked, "When can I move in?" Reiterating that we haven't gotten the keys yet, let alone renovated the house, it was still going to take a few months. We finally got the deed, 6 weeks later, and Matt was right along with us painting, laying flooring in his kitchen, helping us along the way to get his house done. While we were speaking with his lender, we found out we had a few other things to do to get it to pass the loan, we jumped on them, and Matt was able to move in after we closed on the property at $77,500. After paying Ryan back his portion and profit, we made $20,000. What a great start.

Ryan and I flipped 2 more homes, and then I took my proceeds and turned to buying a rental. I went to a private auction and bought a house for $9,000. This was a small, 650sf, 2 bedroom ranch. After putting $9,000 into it for renovations, we rented the house out for $700/mo.

RENTALS

Rentals are a great way to become financially free and get away from corporate America. Our first year buying rentals was slow, we only bought rentals we could buy with cash, put money into, then rent for top dollar. Rentals are tough though, pending the market you are in. The Midwest is the best area we have found to buy and keep rental properties (more on this later.) My best advice to give on rentals is, "If you wouldn't live in the unit you are asking someone else to live in, fix it or do not be a landlord." Rentals, for some, are the lifeblood of their operations. Most millionaires become millionaires through rentals.

ASSET VS INCOME MILLIONAIRE

You can become a millionaire two different ways in real estate. An Asset Millionaire or an Income Millionaire. An asset millionaire strictly has assets (or property) worth a million dollars or more. An income millionaire is a little harder to achieve, although not unobtainable.

Let's say you net (income minus expenses) $200/mo per unit you own. To become a millionaire you have to obtain 417 units all making $200/mo. You will make $83,400/mo net and $1,000,800/yr net.

Now, that's great, but being an income millionaire will take you much longer than acquiring $1,000,000 in assets. For Mid Ohio, where I reside, our average household purchase price is $148,000 (Feb 2022). In order to be an asset millionaire, you have to only own 7 properties. For some locations in the US, you cannot buy a property under $1,000,000, so your purchase number would be 1.

Rentals are a great way to produce income and start paying down debt. What are your goals for getting into real estate? Maybe you want to retire early, send your kids to college, or buy the dream house. Those are all great things, but I challenge you to remember that you have an opportunity to help renters too. Whether it's providing a great home to a tenant, or providing a temporary home to someone who got displaced because of a fire, home owning and having rentals are great ways to benefit the community you invest in. Commercial properties can help tenants start businesses, grow their business, or help a church on Sunday have a place to meet and then during the week be a place for a food pantry. Owning a rental has limitless opportunities.

LONG TERMS VS SHORT TERM RENTALS

Long term rentals are rentals where a tenant stays for longer than 1 month. Most landlords have leases that are for 1 year and then go month to month tenancy after the year. Some landlords like a shorter lease, some only doing month to month leases. Make sure to check with your local laws to which you can provide to your tenants. I typically do a 6 month or a 1 year lease, then we go month to month. If the tenant only wants to do a 6 month lease, I generally will increase the monthly rate by $50/mo simply because I need to put more money back into the property when the tenant moves back out and have to take time to obtain a new tenant. Tenants that are on shorter leases are typically because of their job, think Traveling Nurses or Pipeline Workers, or they are looking to buy a property in the near future and don't want to be locked in for a year and miss being able to buy their new home. Either way, short term leases (6 months) are never a bad thing, just make sure you have it clear in the lease.

Short term rentals are where a tenant stays anywhere from 1 night to 29 nights. Most states, after night 29, will force a landlord to evict a renter. Check with your local laws on how long someone can stay before having to evict them (squatters rights.) Most people know AirBNB, VRBO, etc. These are great resources to get started for making money in short term rentals. There are also managers for short term rentals in tourist cities (Orlando, New York City, etc) that you can use for a fee, but they can keep your property rented and make sure all the fine details are taken care of for you. Details like cleaning the unit after renters, finding renters, and making sure all maintenance issues are handled in a timely manner.

B.R.R.R.R.

BRRRR. No, I'm not cold, even though I live in Ohio. BRRRR is Buy, Rehab (Renovate), Rent, Refinance, Repeat. Brandon Turner from Bigger Pockets originated the term, although it's a common term in real estate now. Thanks Brandon. His podcast partner David Greene wrote a book called "BRRRR- The rental property investment strategy made simple" My first BRRRR property was an oops. Ryan, my private lender, and I bought a property that a lady was selling that she inherited. I was actually heading to look at a new property that hit sheriff sale and passed a homemade sign in the yard 2 doors down. We bought the property from her for $17,000. After renovations of $18,000 ($35,000 all in) we tried to sell it as a flip. The market was not ready for it, or at least the price we wanted for it. I needed to get Ryan paid back, with his interest, and make sure he stayed happy. We pulled the listing and got a renter in for $750/mo. After getting the tenant in, we talked to the bank and refinanced the property. We pulled out enough money to pay Ryan back, with interest, and keep some money in our own pocket. What a great deal, right? After 1 year of having the property as a rental the tenant moved out.

Remember my best advice for a landlord, "If you wouldn't live in the unit you are asking someone else to live in, fix it or do not be a landlord." I'm glad I heeded my own advice. We sold our second house and our new house (new to us) was not ready to move into so we needed to live in our rental for 6 months. We were in a place where we needed a place to live so our rental became our place until our house was ready to move into. Once we were able to move into our other home, we were able to get a tenant into it pretty quick. We have since sold the house and were able to put more cash into our pockets, although looking back now I wish we would've kept the homes we sold, as rentals.

WHOLESALING

Lastly, I want to discuss something that I personally do not do, but I work with them on a weekly basis. Wholesaling. Some states it is illegal to wholesale. Some title companies, we use title companies in Ohio, will not work with wholesalers. It is a very touchy subject, which is why I stay away from it for myself. As a seller's agent my job is to get the most amount of money I can for my seller. As a buyer's agent my job is to get the best deal for my buyer.

As a wholesaler, I'm getting the least amount of money from a seller. See the issue here?

As an agent it is my obligation to help sellers sell properties, and I have a duty to help them get the most they can for the property. If I were to not do this it could turn out bad for me once the property is sold, and the seller finds out I didn't do what was in their best interest. Now, I know agents that do wholesale, and I will not say that I will never wholesale, I just do not at the time of writing this book. If I were to wholesale, it would be in another state as I would not have the same duties to the sellers in the state. I would still advise them what I plan on doing with the property, but I don't have the same duties to them.

Wholesaling is getting a property in contract. Once the property is in contract, I, as the buyer, can sell the contract (via assignment fee) to someone else so long as there is a clause in the contract to do so. Now, I am not selling real estate. I am selling a contract. There is a difference and that difference can land you in serious trouble if caught. Under NAR rules, you cannot sell real estate in the USA without having your real estate license. It does not say you cannot sell a contract without a license, especially if you are selling your interest in the contract. Here is the breakdown on a majority of wholesaling contracts that I see.

Seller and Wholesaler agree to terms on the sale of a property for $100,000. Wholesaler takes pictures and posts the contract for sale to a cash or hard money buyer (we will go into this later) for $125,000. At closing the seller gets their $100,000 (minus fees) and the wholesaler gets $25,000. The end buyer gets the property. The wholesaler has no money in the contract (unless there is earnest money deposit required by the seller, which the wholesaler typically will charge to the buyer.) The wholesaler literally made $25,000 for connecting a buyer and a seller. I've seen some wholesalers make $300,000 plus on an assignment fee, but also have seen them as low as $1,000.

The property value and what the wholesaler can get the property for will be able to determine the assignment fee amount.

Currently, at the time of this writing, I have a buyer that is buying 2 apartment complexes. The wholesaler was actually planning on buying the properties for $900,000. He reached out to me, and asked if I had a buyer as his lender changed terms and he needed to come up with another $100,000, of course I had a buyer. I reached out to a couple investor buyers and one took the deal. My investor buyer agreed to buy the contract for $944,900. Now, the wholesaler had already put money into the deal through inspections and other costs associated with the deal, but he will still make money off of the property. At closing he will take home $44,900, my buyer will have 24 more units and the seller will bring home their proceeds from the sale. I will break down the property later in the book, so don't fret right now about knowing all of the numbers.

Now that we've looked at the different ways to do investing, but believe me, there are many more. From note buying, to seller financing (we will discuss this later), real estate has an endless potential to make money. These are just some of the most popular ones I am comfortable speaking on at this time. Let's look at the best areas to buy real estate in the US.

CHAPTER 2

FINDING YOUR AREA

SO FAR AWAY

You have to do your own research on where you are comfortable with real estate. For me, it's within 25 minutes from my home. I do not own property outside of 25 minutes from my home. I also work with, as a REALTOR®, investors that live all over the US who buy in our area. From California to Maryland, Florida to New Hampshire, we have investors buying property in Mid Ohio. You have to be comfortable with the area you are investing in. You have to look at city growth (shrinkage), crime rates, median income, median age, average purchase price compared to average rental price. For most investors, their comfort level is in the Midwest or south central parts of the US. From the state up north (sorry, can't say it, okay it's Michigan, Go Bucks!) to Alabama. From Western Pennsylvania to Iowa. This area has become a hotspot for investors. There are investors that will only invest in Florida, New York or California.

TIMING

Timing is also a part of where you should choose to invest. Currently, 2022, Texas and Tennessee are hot markets. People are leaving some states and moving to these states. Ohio just got a promise from Intel to create 3,000 jobs in the New Albany area (Northwest of Columbus) which will be huge for the area and will only increase the property values. We are about an hour north of New Albany, and we will see an influx of property values because of this new business. Businesses will come to the area, creating even more jobs simply because of Intel. I was watching the New Albany market prior to Intel's announcement and an acre of land more than 10x the value after the announcement.

SpaceX created an average salary of $107,000 in Brownsville, TX. The area has outgrown itself, and people are buying in adjacent cities because of the SpaceX. Keep an eye out for what company is going where. Those are ideal places for the next investment.

I was looking in Columbus, OH in 2018 for duplexes. I was looking at units near the eastside of Nationwide Children's hospital. At the time a duplex that needed a complete overhaul was going for an average of $80,000. Looking today, the same duplexes are going between $290-599k. The one for $290,000 is in worse condition than I could've bought 4 years ago. Talk about kicking yourself in the butt on that one. But, it wasn't my time to buy $80,000 properties. Now is my time, and Mid Ohio is my place. You'll find your time and your place, do your research and start investing.

TYPE OF PROPERTY

Now let's look at the type of property you are looking to start investing in. We've looked at different types of investing and you know where you want to invest. Now, do you start with single family, multi-family, apartments, or commercial?

SINGLE FAMILY

Single family housing is defined as a house where one family can live. These are the majority of properties in the US. A single family investment can be a solid investment as a rental for the fact that a tenant will make the property their own the longer they live in the house. A tenant will grow a garden, keep the yard mowed, wash windows, plow snow, and make it their property, all while paying you rent. Tenants tend to stay longer in a single family home.

However, there are negatives. I actually just sold the last of my single family homes, besides my own that I live in. The reason I did this was because of the one con that I can think of, that's vacancies. If you have a vacancy on a single family home, you do not have money coming in on the property and the bills still come in. You also do not make as much per month on a single family home as you would a multi-family house.

Say, for example, you have a single family home you bought for $100,000. Now, say your rent is $1,000 per month that you collect. Your PITI comes out to be $700/mo. You net, without any other expenses $300/mo. Now, you have to change the water heater, you are in the negative for a couple months. Roof? Forget it. You won't make that back up for a year. Single Family properties are good if you've taken care of the capex (capital expenditures) issues up front and won't have them for years down the road. When we buy properties, any property, we will go in and replace plumbing, furnace, water heater, flooring (lVP), bathrooms, and kitchen. Should the roof have less than 5yrs left on its life we will replace that as well. Windows, siding, and doors are updated as needed. This will help eliminate major expenses for a few years, barring a tenant doesn't get upset and destroy the place.

MULTI-FAMILY

As mentioned before, we have sold all of our single family and only have multi-family properties. Even though we started out with only single family properties we knew it wasn't a long term play for us. We quickly bought multi-family units.

Here is why. Let's take our same purchase of $100,000 property. On a single family we were only making $300/mo net. Our triplex we just bought ($84,000 purchase and $6,000 renovations) we pay all utilities. We currently rent the three units for a total of $2,500/mo. The PITI is $500/mo and utilities are $800/mo. We end up netting $1,200/mo on this one property. That is 4xs as much as we were making in a single family. We also know the tenants will not stay as long so we will have turnover. Even with the turnover we have, we will still have tenants living there and paying the bills, unless they all move out the same month which is unlikely. This was a deal that I sent all of my investors, ran the numbers for them, and none of them bought it. Once I told one of my investors that has bought multiple properties through me as his realtor, and we have an 18 unit complex together, he was kicking himself for not buying it. It wasn't the right time for him on that deal so he didn't pull the trigger.

APARTMENTS

The 18 unit complex was a smashing deal. Next, I want to discuss apartments. Apartments have their good and bad. We bought the 18 unit property for $415,000 off of another agent in our brokerage. We bought it through seller-financing (will go over later, just keep reading.) Through the use of my investor, let's say his name is Todd, we put down 15% of the purchase price. Our agreement was that he would put another $75,000 into the deal, and I would manage the property, including the rehab. Should we progress further, there is a 3rd floor to the property that we may turn into short term rentals. That's to be discussed down the road. When we first bought the property we had 5 paying tenants for a combined gross income of $2,350/mo. Our monthly payment to the seller was for $2,300/mo. We knew we needed to move fast to get tenants in and get income coming in.

After 3 months, and 5 contractors working on the property, we only had 4 units left to renovate and the income coming in is over 11,200/mo. There are still issues with the property, from cockroaches that an inherited tenant had for over a year before we bought it, to water line breaks after turning them off after being on for so long right after completing the unit.

We still prevail. We still push forward. We still use the same advice, "If you wouldn't live in the unit you are asking someone else to live in, fix it, or do not be a landlord." If I cannot live in the unit, I'm not going to ask someone else to live there. Although there is more money coming in, we still have not taken a dime of income. Todd and I have bigger ideas for the property, and Todd has been great at allowing me to continue to grow the rents, put money back into the property, and increase the value. At some point we will be refinancing the property, pulling cash out, and buying the next complex, but for now, we are buying equity into our current property.

Apartments are a good way to use BRRRR. Another investor, we will call him Tori, bought a property for $655,000. Tory used a hard money lender to purchase and renovate the property. Tory has all in $800,000 between the purchase and renovations. Tory then refinances the property at a value of $1,100,000. Tory can pay off his hard money lender, take back the money he originally put in, and have no cash into the property where he will make $13,000/mo gross.

Apartments are not all glitz and glamor. They have their issues as well. Tenants do not take care of the properties as they do a single family or multi-family. Tenants move in and out faster in apartments. Tenants don't always get along with each other.

COMMERCIAL REAL ESTATE

Lastly, let's talk about Commercial real estate. Commercial real estate is where a property is either a storefront, warehouse, restaurant, etc. Some type of business is going into the property. Some of these may also have apartments above them (called mix-use property.) Commercial properties will typically have a business as the tenant. Commercial deals are nice as the tenant will sign a longer lease. Most times a NNN or Triple Net lease is signed. This is where a tenant will not only pay you rent, but they will pay the property taxes and insurance on the property. The tenants will also pay for their own build out and will take care of their own lawn care and snow removal (should it be needed.) Landlords are typically responsible for the parking lot, exterior lighting, and those types of items, but not always. The nice part of owning the property is you can make your own lease, and you can work with the tenant to make sure everything is taken care of. At the time of this writing I have one commercial property that we are working on rehabbing for a new business we are getting ready to start.

You have decisions to make. What you choose to decide will determine what your next few years look like. You don't have to stick with one decision either. One nice thing about real estate is as long as you own something, you have something you can sell and make money on, if needed. I have an investor client who has bought multiple single family properties. He went outside of his norm and bought an apartment building. After 1 year of owning the building he sold the building and bought more single family homes. He found out quickly that the apartment model was not his niche, and he wanted to stay in his lane.

In the next few chapters we are going to talk about finding the right deal for you. How does that look? How do you market? Where are these "deals" everyone is talking about? Let's move forward together.

CHAPTER 3

GET OUT AND MARKET

FINDING THE DEAL FOR YOU

Getting started, you will find yourself searching high and low for properties. There are many ways you can find a deal. Staying consistent is the number one thing you need to find yourself doing while searching for properties. As my broker, Peter Peterson, wrote in his book, "Contacts=Contracts", "The SSA finds that out of 100 retirees, on average, one retires wealthy, four retire financially secure, five will continue to work, not because they want to, but because they must. Thirty-six will die before retirement and fifty-three will retire broke.

This statistic hangs on the refrigerator in our office break room as a constant reminder of how hard you must work to retire comfortably." A constant reminder of how hard you must work to retire comfortably. Let me repeat that one more time… hard work you MUST work to retire comfortably. Life is not easy. Retiring and living comfortably does not come easy. It doesn't come just by luck. It comes from hard work. Daily grinding. Getting up every morning like everyone else and doing the things you dreaded doing yesterday but no one else will. Rolling out of bed and pounding the pavement. Living today like no one else so you can live tomorrow (your retirement) like no one else. It's easy to say it but not as easy when the rubber meets the road, and you have to live it. We have a few ways that we have seen the best returns for daily grinding and finding the best properties.

MARKETING TO THE MASSES

With social media so prevalent in everyone's life currently, everyone gets marketed to constantly. You can say, "I love the new Real Estate NFT (non-fungible token)" and within 10 minutes you will be bombarded with links to NFT sites. Our phones are some of the most powerful things man has ever created. We can market by just a few clicks from anywhere we have internet service. As an agent, I like using an NFC business card. It's fast, easy, and transfers all the data needed to the other person. You can create your own NFC business card. There is also mass marketing through postcards.

I have received many "I will buy your property in cash" postcards every week. Most times these are wholesalers trying to get a hold of you, but sometimes it's a landlord looking to buy their next property. Either way, this is a good, inexpensive, way to get out to the masses in one shot. Right now you can buy real estate postcards for $0.45 each. So, if you bought 1000 and sent them to a neighborhood, with stamps, addresses, etc, you may have $1.00 each card you send out. If 1 person calls you on from those flyers, you could potentially more than 5x your money. That's just from one person calling you back. Even if you don't hear anything from the first round, keep showing up. Send a second round but narrow it down more to maybe vacant homes, or homes where the owner doesn't live at the property. You will learn about doing this type of marketing a little further down.

KNOCK, KNOCK

The next type of marketing is the best type of marketing. Face to Face. Getting in front of a potential seller and talking to them. This can be done in a few ways. Door knocking is my favorite. Find a neighborhood that you want to invest in for your next properties. Whether it's a rental or flip, you now know what you want to get into. Multi-million dollar properties are few and far between in Mansfield, OH to hope to buy as a rental. That's not going to be a smart investment as you begin. You may however go to a neighborhood with multiple multi-family properties where homes range between $70,000 and $150,000 to find a rental. Start knocking. No one home? Leave a card. Mark on a spreadsheet what homes you spoke to, who was not home, who was interested in further pursuing selling, who was not, and if the property was vacant. The homes you spoke to and may be interested, follow up next week, or sooner. Stay in front of their face. Drop them a postcard with interest in buying their home. Drop a business card in their door. By the third visit, you should know their dog's name and bring the dog a treat. The key here is consistency.

Like all marketing, stay in front of the person you are trying to sell to. Now, you are thinking, "Adam, I'm not selling, I'm buying properties." You are correct, but you are selling yourself that you are the best person to buy their property. Sell yourself. Let them know your plans for the property, if you know already, and how you are going to take care of the property.

For most people who are living in the property, they are going to sell it as an investment for them and they have time, sweat, blood, tears in their home. They don't want it to just be another blip on the map in a couple years because some investor came in and ruined their pink shag carpet. Don't lie to them but also don't go so in depth with what your plans are that they do not want to sell to you. Sell the vision for the property to them.

While face to face with a potential seller, keep an eye out for a potential buyer for that property as well. Remember, you can flip the property right in front of you quickly if you already have a buyer lined up. Keep an open eye and ear out for buyers for yourself.

Maybe this type of marketing is not for you, do not stop reading. Get help finding properties and you can even get help managing the properties. I can help you make all the needed connections during the buying, property managing, and selling processes in Ohio, or find another local real estate agent outside of Ohio. The purpose of this book is to help educate and empower you to take the next step. I'm happy to help you along your journey whether it is just reading my book, or if it's using my networking and skills to serve you all throughout your journey.

DRIVING FOR $$$$$

Have you ever gone driving to a friend's house that just moved, and you're listening to music in the car? While you get close to your friend's new house, you turn the radio down? Why did you do that? Most likely it was so you can concentrate on finding where your friend lives. The same thing with the next way to find deals. Driving for dollars. Pick a neighborhood. Any neighborhood you want to market for properties. Drive up and down every road, alley, side street you can find and look for that friend. The one, or two, or multiple houses that are vacant. Write the address down. Keep driving until you find the next one.

Once you finish driving the neighborhood and scaring the neighbors because you are creeping on empty houses, head home. Make sure the cops are not following you, and if they are just pull over and let them know what you are doing and that you are trying to make the neighborhood a better place to live. Once home, and some people can do it right from their phone, search "driving for dollars." You will find multiple apps or websites dedicated just for helping you find the owner of the vacant house. If you know it's a rental, maybe it's a multi family property, use that address as well. You have your list, and you can put it in the system. Within seconds this system will spit out all the information you need to start calling potential sellers. Some that I have used have up to 10 potential phone numbers and up to 5 emails. Call every one of those numbers and email every email until you get the owner.

Once again, if this does not sound like something you would see yourself doing, I have connections that can help. We have a team in place to help you from start to millionaire. My wife and I have done this to find deals for my network of investors. I connect with wholesalers to also find deals like this too.

CONSTANT CONTACT

Now it's time to build and make the next contact. Keep contacting them until they sell you the property. Don't be annoying, but be helpful. Be willing to take your time with them. It may have been a property that their mom was living in and has just passed away, and they now don't know what to do with it. Be consistent but be sympathetic to them as you need. But always be willing to help. Helping them will go a long way in your journey.

VIRTUAL ASSISTANT

Now that you have built more and more lists, your time is valuable but you can't be in multiple places at once. It's time to bring on an assistant. One type of assistant that we like to use are Virtual Assistants (VA). A VA can help you with multiple tasks. From cold calling to setting appointments to building your website to creating and sending postcards. VA's can give you time back now that you have built this empire of a pipeline. There are multiple locations where you can find a quality VA. Some people like to keep it in the USA. There are call centers in the US that specialize in virtual assistants. These companies charge anywhere from $25-50 per hour, pending what all you need.

The VA's that I like to use are actually in the Philippines. A VA in the Philippines will cost me significantly less than in the US. Most VA's that I have spoken with have some type of higher education, while some are programmers. You can find a VA in the Philippines for ⅓ the price as you can in the USA, which is why some companies use them compared to staying in the states. Another nice thing, a Filipino can speak English almost as well as Americans, but with a slight accent.

Lastly, on finding deals, we use scripts for every contact we make on the phone or through email. Each script is laid out in such a way that we either get the contract, a second contact, or three "no's." We always follow up in a timely manner should we get a second contact request. We always follow up if we get three "No's." Just because someone says, "no" at this point, does not mean it's No forever. Keep them on the backburner and don't forget about them. Contacts=Contracts. Keep contacting, but don't be pushy. No one likes a pushy person. Keep grinding. No's are hard but each No will lead you to the next yes.

CHAPTER 4

WHERE ARE THE DEALS?

WHERE ARE THE DEALS?

Deals can come in many forms. I have seen deals come across my desk many different ways and I have worked hard to get deals in front of me. I've called, emailed, stopped by the house, called again, all to get the deal done. But what are some other ways you can find a deal?

MLS

The Multiple Listing Service is a great way to find deals. These are active sellers who we know want to sell. How do we know they want to sell? They listed their property for sale through a Real Estate agency. The Multiple Listing Service (MLS) is used by REALTORS ® in each Board of Realtors. Ohio currently, at the time of this publication, has 32 local associations and boards. With so many localized boards, finding a property for you should be easier. Hire a REALTOR ® and let them help you find properties.

POCKET LISTINGS

Along with the MLS, your real estate agent can help you find what is called a pocket listing in their brokerage. These are listings that are not on the MLS market but the seller is still wanting to sell them. These can be gold mines for the right person to come along and make a decent offer to the seller. Your agent should help you find off market pocket listings.

SHERIFF SALE

Sheriff sales are great once you understand the process. Shortly after the crash of 2008, there were hundreds of thousands of properties going to sheriff sale, some at pennies on the dollar. Banks couldn't keep up with them. The owners couldn't keep up with them. In our county, Richland county, the sales of multiple properties every week lasted well into 2019. Eleven years after the "crash" we were still seeing thirty plus properties going to sheriff sale. Now, you are wondering, what is a sheriff sale?

A sheriff sale is when a lienholder has declared foreclosure and the property has been repossessed. There is a default in the loan or on property taxes. There are court hearings on the process but we will skip that part and get to the actual sale and what you will look at in all of this.

The sheriff will post all properties for sale three weeks prior to the auction. This is a must. Most times, especially now, they will have it listed on their websites with the court number, the address, auction starting price, and the current market value (based on the auditor's website.) You, as the buyer, can drive by the property as soon as you see the property is going to auction. DO NOT ENTER. You are considered trespassing. You can evaluate the deal of each property, which we will get into in the next chapter. For sheriff sales, assume the worst, pray for the best. Assume you are going to have to replace cabinets, flooring, paint, HVAC, water heaters, electrical, plumbing, roof, siding, windows, and doors. Obviously, you can see a few of these items, but make sure your numbers reflect the replacement of everything inside. If you get the property, and it's not in that bad of shape, you just gave yourself a raise. You can also search it online or at the clerk of courts. You can find anything from, what the previous owner bought it for, what liens were on the property that went through the courts, and much more. If you really want a property and want to make sure all liens are known, do a title search through your title company or an attorney's office.

Time for the sale. You've done your research, you know what you can bid on each property at the sale. Let's start bidding. Since the pandemic hit in 2020 most, if not all, sheriff sales have gone to online bidding. This is good and bad. Good as you can stick to your numbers and not worry about getting caught in the moment and saying, "just one more thousand should get them to stop." I've done one more thousand bids and have over paid on properties. Fortunately, I still made out on them but it can be bad if not kept in check.

You won your property. You still do not own the property. You cannot kick out the tenant, mow the lawn, or replace a lightbulb. Wait. You have to wait for the sheriff to give you a sheriff's deed, which typically takes 6-8 weeks but sometimes takes longer. I have seen this take years to receive. Unfortunately for you, you don't get your money back because you are waiting too long. If there is a tenant in place, then you can start the eviction process. I have done cash for keys, where I paid them the going rent rate to leave by X date, on a few deals where there is a tenant in place, and I didn't want them there. It's much cheaper than eviction in the long run, especially if they are angry people and you think they will destroy the place.

Sheriff sales can be a good place to get a cheap property, even if you plan on moving into them. We go into more discussion on our video at Dreamhugedeals.com. You can find more helpful resources and my hot list of deals at that website.

FOR SALE BY OWNER

A third way to find the deal is through For Sale By Owner (FSBO.) As you are driving for dollars, or just taking a stroll down the sidewalk in the neighborhood you live in, you will see FSBO signs in yards. These signs are great ways to get into the house and make sure it's a good fit for your investment portfolio. Call the number on the sign, show up at the right time, or knock on the door if you know they are home. Either way you have a willing and able seller.

FSBO will oftentimes try to sell on their own prior to listing with a real estate agent. Most often the list price on the home is either too high or too low. If it is too low and it is still for sale, their marketing was not done correctly. They may have just put the sign in the yard and hoped and prayed that it would sell. If it is listed too high, you can help them with getting it sold… to you.

FSBO can be tough as most sellers have never sold a house before. They don't know the contracts, they don't know the steps to selling, they don't know whether to use an attorney or title company (every state is different so be sure to look up what you use in the state you are buying.) Most sellers do not know about Earnest Money, Property Disclosures, or Lead Based Paint disclosures. You, or your agent, will have to teach the seller along the way. Make sure to use an agent you trust to help you. The seller may not pay them their commission, but make sure to take care of them at closing.

WHOLESALING

We talked about wholesaling previously, but I bring it up again as wholesalers can bring good deals to the table as well. I have bought a few properties recently from a wholesaler. I have sold properties that a wholesaler has brought me to my end buyers. Wholesalers do the majority of the marketing for you already, but don't worry not everyone will sell to them but want to sell to you. Wholesalers will help you find deals and work together to make each other money. If you are truly wanting to find the best deals that are not on market and make sure all deals are brought before you, make sure your real estate agent works alongside a wholesaler. Wholesalers connect with each other and will even "JV" a deal together to get it done. JVing a deal is when one wholesaler has the property in contract but another wholesaler brings the buyer. The two wholesalers split the fee that is associated with the contract. It's really a win/win/win for everyone. The wholesalers each make some money and the investor, you, can get a great property for less than it being on the market.

I bought a recent duplex from a wholesaler. I bought the duplex for $34,000. The wholesaler had the property in contract for $25,000. He made $9,000 off of the deal. For me, it was a win. I now have the property rented for $1,000/mo after putting $5,000 into the renovations. For him it was a win because he made $9,000 for taking some pictures and advertising the property. For the seller it was a win because they were able to sell the property for what they wanted to sell it for.

By now you have determined what you want to do to grow your real estate investing career. You have preyed on a neighborhood and know what each house should sell for if the property is in its best shape and best use. You have scoured through for sale and sold comps to find the right neighborhood to market. You have used your real estate agent to find you deals, while looking for deals through other streams. Now we can move into the nitty gritty in evaluating the deal. This is where I geek out, so bear with me.

CHAPTER 5

EVALUATING THE DEAL

The next step in creating a solid real estate portfolio is evaluating the deal. Real estate agents and investors like to use a few different avenues for making sure a deal is truly a deal. I should note not all real estate agents understand these concepts, so make sure you get with an investor friendly realtor like myself. I will break down the process and give a few examples for you to make it quick and easy to see a deal fast or to run away. A few of these are solely for rentals while others are solely for flipping/BRRRR and now that you know which route you want to take in investing (maybe it's all 3 of them), you can easily determine which evaluation you want to execute in your search for the next deal. Let's dive into a few of them.

1% RULE FOR RENTALS

The 1% Rule (or guide) is the number one guide that helps investors determine if a property is a good deal for a rental. The guide is very simple. The 1% rule states that the sale price of a property should be determined by at least being able to rent the property for 1% of the sale. For example: a $100,000 property should rent for a minimum of $1,000.

This guide has helped me determine what is a good deal real fast, and be able to put a property in contract shortly after hitting the market. My last deal was a triplex in a small town called Galion, OH. This triplex was listed for sale for $99,900. The next day I sent an offer for $99,000. The seller accepted. I knew with it being a triplex the tenants there were at least paying $333 each. Once in contract, I was able to go through the property and evaluate what repairs were needed, speak with tenants, and get leases to know for sure what the rents are currently. The rent amount was for $1250/mo. Gross rent. This was not quite the homerun I was used to as previous purchases that were for a similar price but gross rents equal $2500/mo. However, I proceeded with the purchase knowing that when the tenants were no longer on leases I would be increasing rents to actual market rents. Traditionally, we like to at least hit 1.5% for our deals and will not send a deal to an investor to purchase unless it hits this number.

The 1% rule is simply a guide to make a fast decision for a sale price, when purchasing a rental. There are some larger cities, or areas where appreciation is increasing at a rapid pace and the 1% rule will not apply, so it might look like a bad deal. However, investors will still buy the property. Why? Investors are banking on significant appreciation in the future. Columbus Ohio is a great example of this. Remember my example earlier? I could have bought a property for $80,000 that is now worth over $300,000? The appreciation exploded in just a few years.

NOI

Net Operating Income (NOI) is our next deal evaluation. This evaluation can be for a rental or a flip. Investopia states that, "To calculate NOI, subtract all operating expenses incurred on a property from all revenue generated on the property. The operating expenses used in the NOI metric can be manipulated if a property owner defers or accelerates certain income or expense items. The NOI metric does not include capital expenditures." Pretty simple, right? Let's break it down on an easy flip deal we did recently.

We bought the property for $415,000. This is the 18 unit complex I spoke of earlier in the book. Due to the improvements completed, currently our rent roll brings in $11,200 every month in rent, which easily brings in the 1% rule we just spoke of, and soon we will be adding a laundromat in the building to help bring in more income, but right now, this is all of our current income. Our monthly expenses average is $5,300. Multiplied over a yearly basis, our NOI is $70,800. Your basis on what a good NOI is for you will determine what you are wanting to make in the property.

CAP RATE

Third on our list for evaluating a deal, falling in line with how we evaluate a property, is Capitalization Rate (Cap Rate). Cap rates are calculated by dividing the property's net operating income (NOI) from its property asset value, traditionally the list price.

Using the 18 unit property, our Cap rate for the property is found by taking the $70,800 NOI and dividing it by $525,000 (the $415k purchase and $110k rehab), or a 13.4% Cap Rate. A "good" cap rate is between 8-12%.

So far we have found that a 1% deal is a good "start." From there, breaking down the property to find the NOI is next. Finding the cap rate after figuring the NOI to determine where the deal stands by taking the NOI and dividing it by the purchase price (because you may not know the rehab amount yet.) Most buyers will find and add the rehab amount into the purchase price to get the most accurate Cap rate. The next step is finding the Return on Investment.

RETURN ON INVESTMENT

The Return on Investment (ROI) of an investment is traditionally calculated with a flip property, and not a rental. The ROI is found by taking the sale price of the property and subtracting the cost of the purchase and rehab on the property. Once you get this number, divide it by the total purchase and rehab cost of the property. For example:

I purchased a house through auction for $22,000. My renovation costs came out to $16,000. With $38,000 all in, I sold the property for $65,000. After everything was completed, I brought home $23,500, due to taxes, title, and commissions. The ROI was 71%. A "good" ROI is around 15% but I do not send investors anything that would come in under 20% ROI.

CASH ON CASH RETURNS

We can break a deal down further and figure out my Cash on Cash return, which is another way to evaluate a property. Cash on Cash (CoC) is a wonderful way to figure out what you bring home compared to what you have into a property. Let's say I took a loan from a Hard Money Lender (HML) for the property mentioned. The HML charges me a rate of 8% (this is on the low end, but I have been doing this a while, so they're giving me a great rate.) My monthly hold on the property paying interest only is $253 per month. It took us 6 months to rehab and sell the property once we purchased it. My lender required me to put 15% down on the property at the time of purchase but paid for the entire renovation. My money out of pocket is $3,300 plus closing costs, which was a sheriff auction so there was only $150 closing costs. All in, I have $3,450 on the property. I sold the property for $65,000. After paying the lender back his $34,700, I am left with the profit of $22,032. Taking out commissions, taxes, title fees, I was left with $17,500. This property gave me a CoC return of 507%.

This is a low level property with minimal cash into the deal, but with a larger property, your CoC will be much, much less. The average CoC return is between 8-12%, with 10% being a "good" investment. I like to bring CoC deals of 25% to our investors as this will allow them to make the profits they need to grow and expand.

CHAPTER 6

WHO'S GOT MY MONEY?

I like Grant Cardone. He is the loud mouth, controversial, billionaire that is always in your inbox trying to get you to buy his next conference. He does a 10X growth conference every year where tens of thousands attend and millions watch online. At our office, we have watched the last two conferences on our big screen, with everyone invited to learn. He brings onto the stage successful people who help teach you how they began, most with simpler lives just like you and I. He is also the only Undercover Billionaire that built a company worth $5 million in 90 days, so he knows a thing or two about real estate. He is always talking about, "Who's got my money?" Who in your group of influence has money that you can get, whether it's through buying something or them lending it to you. I love the saying, but we are going to discuss it a little differently than Mr Cardone.

We've discussed a little bit about lenders, but there are more ways than just going to a bank and hoping they will lend to you. Even if you have had a foreclosure, missed payments, or delinquent card card debit in the past, there are options for you too. In this chapter, we will take a look at multiple sources of income and find the best way for you to obtain money. These are just a few options that I have used, but there are more ways than what we will discuss in the book.

SELLER FINANCE

Sellers are great ways to get a loan. Using Seller-Financing is the best way without using a bank to get a loan. The problem with seller-financing is that sellers do not know how it works, so therefore, it scares them. Seller-financing is when the seller becomes the bank and covers the loan amount needed to purchase the property. I have used, and currently use, seller financing to get a deal completed. One of the good things about seller-financing is the buyer and seller can determine how to structure the note (mortgage.) More about this in the last chapter where we dive into our first deal.

BANK LOANS

Secondly, the behemoth lender, the bank. Banks are great when you need them and they are willing to give you money. Banks typically give out loans that you have heard about. For example, FHA, VA, USDA, Conventional, Commercial, 203K, and more.

We have an excellent commercial lender at a local area bank. I first started using them a few months ago and since then we have done 2 lines of credit on houses that I owned free and clear, and we have purchased 9 rentals, using the lines of credit as down payments. This bank considers anything that is a rental as a commercial loan, even single family.

This is huge as you don't have to deal with traditional conventional loan processes to get a loan approved. I gave my lender tax returns, my current rent roll with each property, and my most recent commission statements. As a real estate agent I work 1099. This makes it very difficult to get traditional loans, without 150 pages of paperwork to fill out and turn in. We are closing on our new house tomorrow (as I write this chapter), and we used traditional conventional loans. We couldn't use our commercial lender, because it was a home we are going to live in, but we are turning our current home into a rental. We bought our current home for $20,000 three years ago. We just had it appraised for $195,000. By adding a fourth bedroom, we were able to move our comps out of our current neighborhood and into a more affluent neighborhood. We were originally going to keep our house as a rental for $1200/mo, but we met a couple that we knew to sell the house to. They are our current associate pastor and youth director.. We turned a $20,000 purchase, $50,000 rehab into a $150,000 sale with no capital gains due to us living there for 2 of the last 5 years. With all this said, using our commercial lender we have been able to really start to scale our portfolio and we are going to continue to grow with them in the near future.

PRIVATE LENDERS

Our third lender is a Private Lender. I spoke briefly about a hard money lender in the previous chapter, but let's dive into more options for private lending now. Private money lenders are not banks but rather persons or companies that loan investors the capital they need to finance their real estate investment deals. Private real estate lenders can do up to a 30 year loan and will most times lend on the renovation costs.

I have one investor right now using hard money lenders for an apartment complex he just bought last month. He is in the process of buying two more next month. With his hard money lender, he was able to put 15% down on each property and his lender would pay the remaining balance on the property while also paying for the renovations. While working on the property, our investor is increasing rents, bringing in better tenants, and increasing his ROI. Using a higher cap rate when he needs to refinance, within 18 months of time of purchase, he will increase the value enough to pay back his lender, take back his initial investment, and pull some cash out for the next deal. These three deals I found for him, and we will be increasing his portfolio very rapidly in the near future.

FRIENDS AND FAMILY

The last group of people we are going to discuss are the hardest group to get to buy into your adventure. They are the ones that want you to succeed but don't, or can't, help you get there. This group is known as your friends and family.

Family and friends are always there for you until you start talking about what you do as an investor. Don't worry, they just don't know and weren't taught how to invest in real estate. Most were taught to put your money in a 401K and retire after your 30 years at a job. Let me halt there.

I dislike jobs. I think we as a society have gotten so far away from where we should be that we are now teaching kids, at a young age, that you have to have a job to be successful and if you work hard enough you can retire at the age of 62 then live the rest of your life on the beach somewhere. I dislike this concept, A LOT. I really wish we would teach our kids about life and investing. Maybe not all real estate investing, but turning your money into more money and letting it work for you, instead of you working for your money. Let's look at the parable of the talents that Jesus taught us about in the Bible.

In Matthew 25 starting in verse 15, Jesus tells a story about a rich man who was heading out on a journey. He would be gone a long time, and he gave three of his servants gold. The first servant got 5 bags of gold, the second got 2 bags of gold, and the third got one bag of gold. The first servant went and "put his money to work", otherwise known as investing. He invested his money. The second did the same and the third hid his bag in the ground. After the rich man came back, the first servant came to him, pleased with himself and said, "I doubled your money." The second did the same, but the third servant brought back his one bag of gold that the rich man gave him. The rich man was upset with him and took his gold from him and gave it to the man with ten bags of gold. Why? If it's anything like this time in our country, it's because due to inflation the rich man lost money by burying it. But seriously, even in the Bible it talks about investing, and how that is a good thing to do with your money. It doesn't say how the first servant made the money, but I like to imagine it was invested in real estate or a start up business. When you invest your money and make smart decisions, there is an opportunity to do more of what you want to do with your time. Invest back into your family, local charities, and community.

Back to our regularly scheduled program. Most citizens in our society do not know how to invest in real estate. Hopefully, they are reading this book and will realize it's not as difficult as they make it sound. Start small, learn along the way, and slowly over time grow. You don't have to buy the next apartment complex to hit the market or the next skyscraper. It can be a single family or duplex. It can be something you do as a part time gig and let a property manager handle the day to day operations. Whatever you do, just start. If you don't want to start, which I don't know why you're still reading this book, then help someone else that does want to start. That, in itself, is a form of real estate investing. Help them get the cash for the down payment on a rental property. Help them pay for a single family flip and get your return, then help again. 29% of homes in the US have no mortgage on them. Think of the equity in those homes and the power they possess, all tax free and can help you grow.

CHAPTER 7

HIRE SLOW. FIRE FAST

This chapter is near and dear to my heart. It's also one of the hardest parts in the process to get correct. Coming from a construction background, I understand this chapter more than some of the others in the book. In this chapter we will discuss Contractors , handymen, and trades people. You can have a contractor for years and all of the sudden they fall off the face of the earth. It's tough. There are also projects where you have to fire multiple contractors because of their lack of commitment. We had to do this on one particular project early on when we first started.

We bought a property for dirt cheap… actually less than dirt because it was on 2 acres as well and you couldn't buy the land for the price we paid for it. We bought it for $10,000. It was a sheriff sale. I absolutely love sheriff sale properties, if you couldn't tell from chapter 4. The suspense of not knowing what is behind the door. Back to our property we just closed and got the deed for cheap dirt.

Shortly after closing, I was approached by a mennonite man who asked me to buy the property. I should have sold it then, but looked at the numbers and didn't want to miss out on extra money sitting on the table. I had run the numbers, and we were ready to rake in on some cash. I brought an investor along with me, not because we needed the cash to pay for the purchase, but to help pay for the rehab. It was a complete gut, one of the ones I told you about in chapter 4 where everything needed touched. The farmhouse was a 3 bedroom, 1 bathroom 2 story. It already had a metal roof but the roof leaked. There was a family of raccoons we had to evict. There was so much raccoon feces in the house you couldn't take a step without stepping on it.

We found our first contractor, we will name him Carter. He is licensed, insured, and has contracts ready. Carter came in at a good price to do the renovations we wanted. We gave a deposit of $6,000, and he gave us a time-frame of 6 weeks to complete the job. To help Carter along, I also had some handymen type workers that helped do some of the easier items so the contractor could focus on the harder jobs. We added bathrooms, new plumbing, electrical, moved walls, and did all new siding. I would visit daily, and we saw some quick progress up front. After a few weeks progress slowed down. We didn't see as much progress, and Carter wasn't there as often as he had been the first week. Third, fourth week I kept going there and then started asking him where he was. Carter would say he got stuck at another job because his workers needed him, etc etc. Six weeks go by, nothing else is done. Actually, nothing was officially done. Carter was fired and complained that it was my workers fault, or that it was somehow my fault that he didn't show up.

A week goes by and contractor number two, we will call him Sam, comes to save the day. He was referred to us by a family member who he did work for so we thought he would be good. We learned that we were no longer going to pay upfront anything until we saw progress. He lived more than an hour away so asked if during the week he could stay at the house. He could work longer hours and get more work done in a shorter period of time. They started out strong, again. Removing some of the issues the first contractor did but didn't do correct. Then after another three weeks, progress slowed down again. We started seeing things around the property that we knew were not there before. We asked Sam about it, and it was blamed on his partner, Frank. After 6 more weeks, we fired Sam. He went ballistic. He actually grabbed a hatchet and went after his partner. I stopped him at the door, and talked him off the ledge. He grabbed his items and left that day, bed and all. After doing research, again my workers were still helping as needed, Frank was the one that we could tell was actually doing the work so we hired him and kept him on for 4 more weeks. One thing led to another and he had to go. The items that we kept finding around the property showed up again, and this time we knew who it was.

Contractor number four brought a crew for one day, and we let them go. Finally contractor number five, we will call him Ben. Ben got us almost to completion. We are now almost one year after we originally bought the property. Our short term capital gains taxes were now moved to long term capital gains. Ben was an older retired guy who worked construction his whole life and now just does it for fun. Ben found some issues that should have been caught after contractor one but weren't and everyone else missed them or decided it wasn't their job. Fortunately, Ben caught it and was able to get it corrected in a timely manner.

Contractors are tough. They will lie, steal, cheat, take short cuts, and do just about anything to get paid without doing work. Unless you find a Ben. Find a Ben on your crew. Someone whose word is his bond and he will take care of the project from start to finish and not cut corners, not charge an arm or leg, and be upfront with you.

REMODELING- WORTH THE PRICE?

You have hopefully gone through this step but the most difficult part of real estate is determining what to renovate and when. Your contractor should be able to help you with this step. They should be able to walk the property with you prior to closing to get you a quote for labor and materials. Ask them to split the prices. Do your own research on materials. Are they charging you more than double the cost for materials? At this point in time, most contractors should not have to go into the store and pick up materials. Almost all stores now deliver, and the fee is very reasonable. The contractor can even send the store the list, and they will get the pricing together, set up multiple delivery times to not have all materials delivered at once, and make sure you get everything needed. There is no reason for a contractor to charge double what it costs you to buy that same material, simply because they are ordering it. I actually will not allow my contractors to pay for materials. I ask them for a list, and I will order it and bring it to them, or I will have it delivered. For one, I know what is being ordered, and if they are blowing through materials and not getting anything done, there's a problem. Secondly, it gives me a chance to make time to go check on the project.

Contractors should be able to save you time. Time is money. A good contractor should be able to quickly let you know if a property will be a $4,000 renovation or a $140,000 renovation, without fully running the numbers for the quote. Do not let a contractor walk a property with you without asking them for a rough estimate. Don't hold them to that number, but they also shouldn't come to you with a quick $4,000 verbal estimate, and then quote you $20,000.

I had a contractor once give me a quote for a project of new plumbing, paint, countertops, a few new cabinets, and change out a couple light fixtures for $900 for labor with a two week timeframe. I thought that was very inexpensive so I went with him. Like usual I was there daily checking in. Daily he was there and multiple other people were there. Painters were there, plumbers were there, electricians were there. After seeing how fast the painters were, we asked them to do a few more rooms. I knew this would add a little more to our cost. The contractor was done, and we inspected it and everything was good, until we got the bill. He billed us $3,650. When I asked him why the price was three times what he quoted us, he said, "It cost me more in labor than expected." He also said he had to pay for materials but could never come up with receipts, which I was willing to pay. I ended up paying the painters and plumber directly.

Make sure to always get quotes in writing, and all payments and receipts from contractors. If you do not have something in writing it turns into a "he said, she said" and nothing gets accomplished. Fortunately, I speak to most of my contractors through messaging so I know exactly what was said and can fall back on it should anything be needed later. Obviously, while at the property you can't have a stenographer with you at all times, although that could be fun and scary, but make sure to follow it up with a message repeating everything of importance. The scope of work, costs, when the contractor will get a draw, and whatever else you spoke on that was of importance pertaining to the property. It will save you in the long run.

CHAPTER 8

PM ME

PROPERTY MANAGER FOR THE WIN

Property Managers are amazing and finding a good property manager is worth their weight in gold. There are a select few in our area and the one I refer my investors to takes really good care of them. A good property manager can, and should, make you money.

A good property manager is not just there to collect rents, although that is a small part of their job. They will also get good tenants in place for you. They will suggest renovations that are needed on your property. Property Managers should have maintenance crews on the ready should there be issues at your property. They are the ones that will get the 2am wake up calls for water bursting, and it's raining on the tenants bed. They should be able to have your property rented at market rents within a certain amount of time once it is ready. Property Managers should be able to sift through tenant applications to find the right tenant for your property. Again, collecting rent is just the tip of the iceberg of what a good property manager will do for you.

We have one year leases on all of our properties, then the tenant goes month to month until move out. I self-manage all of our properties currently, as all of our properties are within 25 minutes of my house. When I hit a certain point where I am spending too much time doing other things and not managing my properties correctly, I will pass off the properties to my property management company I mentioned above. But, for now, I can handle the stresses and worries of the day to day.

When we take over a property with a tenant in place, we make sure to introduce ourselves to the tenant and build rapport with them. You do not want to be their friend. You are there to be their landlord. Stick to what their lease says. Do not stray from that. We want their buy-in that their rents are too low (if they are too low) so when I take over and have to increase their rent, they aren't banging down our door but understand the reasoning why. Which again takes me back to our motto, "If you wouldn't live in the unit you are asking someone else to live in, fix it, or do not be a landlord." I make sure the tenant knows that the reason we are raising rents is so we can put even more money into their unit. We aren't raising their rent just to buy that second home on the lake. We want to take care of our tenants. We want to make sure they are comfortable and living their best life, in our properties. Obviously, it's a business and is treated as such, but you have to look at people as well. They are people like you and I who want a good life. If we can give them a good place to live, take care of the small things for them in the property, and make sure to assist where needed, they'll keep renting from us. I have multiple tenants advise they will not move unless I sell the property, and then they'll move into another unit of mine. When you work alongside your tenants, you'll have tenants for the life of the property.

I worked with an investor, Jon, who owns 250 units. I worked with Jon for over a year. When I first started working alongside Jon as a partner, Jon had an occupancy rate of 64%. Jon was breaking even on his properties, barely. Jon was banking on making his money through the laundromat, which was worn down and hardly used. When Jon would refinance a property, he would pocket the cash and live on that until he could refinance another property. It was a losing battle for him. Jon's son, Tom, asked me to help Jon out. I did. I came in and the three of us partnered to make Jon, and everyone money. Through rehabbing empty units, getting the easier ones done first and rented at top dollar, and selling off the properties that need too much work, Jon slowly started making cash. After 1 year of rehabbing, selling, and getting rents at market rents, Jon started to see cash flow. His 64% occupancy rate went up to 92% when I left. This is the same thing your property manager should be able to do for you. They should easily keep a high occupancy rate. 92% is a standard, and I would work with your manager to help them get that rate.

Turnaround time on a unit plays a major role in your occupancy rate. Did a previous tenant get evicted, and now you have to renovate the entire unit, drywall and all? Does it smell like cat urine? Do you have to turn the key and let the next tenant move in? These are things that you should consider when looking at a good property manager and evaluating the job they are doing for you. Not only should your property manager keep your units as full as possible, but they should be able to get your units back on the market as fast as possible. Having their own maintenance and/or construction crews ready to go to get the units turned will make your job easier. Some managers will ask for funds up front to turn a unit, and some will ask on the back end. It really depends on your manager and what you have set up with them. Again, they are there to help you make money, so pay them the extra bit to change out the worn out carpet and freshen the paint. Let them decide when it's time to buy a new vanity and toilet. Do you need granite countertops? New cabinets? New windows and doors? Anything over a certain dollar amount, my amount is $100, should go through you for approval, but do not inhibit what they are trying to do. If you can afford new flooring throughout and they believe it will get a better tenant in place, do it. If you can afford new windows and doors and they believe it'll be more cost efficient for the tenant's utilities, do it. If you can afford a new driveway, put one in. Your new tenants will thank you for not having their vehicles beat up with the potholes.

CHAPTER 9

LAWYER UP

Sometimes things do not go as planned. You always need a backup plan in place before going into something. If not, things can go downhill fast, and you will lose your shirt. This is where a good attorney can come into play. Not only for the bad times but in the good times as well. In this chapter, we will discuss how to look for a good attorney, and why you need a good real estate attorney. There are 5 things to look for in an attorney.

When you want to spend money, saving money is top priority (unless you just hit the lottery and want to just spend it away.) A good real estate attorney can save you money. But Adam, attorney's cost money, how are they going to save me money? A good real estate attorney will review all of the documents and make sure that your investment is safeguarded. Along with real estate agents, attorneys will know what questions to ask when it pertains to the contract to make sure you are safe for closing.

How many deals will you close in your lifetime? Unless you are a licensed real estate agent or an investor that buys or sells properties every week, your attorney will have already done more deals and seen more contracts than you will in your lifetime. With this, they have the knowledge and understanding to make sure everything that is needed in the contract is there and you will be safe to meet at the closing table.

With experience and savings comes clarity. Your attorney will have a clear understanding of what the contract says and can adjust accordingly to make it in your best interest. Your attorney will help make the contract easier to understand. They will be able to speak to you at the level you'll understand and be able to assist in understanding the items you do not understand.

Ohio does not require an attorney to be present at closing, although some states do. Ohio is a title state, and each title company is owned, and all contracts are reviewed by an attorney. Title companies will have standard contracts on hand if your agent does not have one, and they will gladly assist in getting the deals to completion for you. Even with that, you will still want your attorney to assist in making sure everything that you want in the contract is there. The closing table is your last chance to ask questions before taking possession. If you have questions and did not ask before signing, you may be missing things that you didn't know you were missing.

So, attorneys will help you with clarity, savings, experience, closing, and lastly they will assist with protection. Your attorney works for you. They are there for you when you need them. They are not mind readers though. If you have a question, you need to feel confident in asking your attorney for help. Let them assist you in making a great decision and do not go into a contract blindly.

Understanding that not all attorneys are made equal, as with title companies and real estate agents, you'll learn what to look for when seeking out legal advice with real estate transactions. A real estate attorney needs to know the ins and outs of real estate, and them being real estate investors helps make sure they have the knowledge. Let them guide you as you get started in investing. Ask questions, listen for answers, ask them to repeat the things you need to understand but do not understand.

CHAPTER 10

ROUNDING OUT YOUR TEAM

"Surround yourself around four millionaires, and you'll be the fifth. Surround yourself around four junkies, and you'll be the fifth."- Unknown

DETAILS ARE IN THE TITLE

Title is a wonderful resource to have for a real estate investor. In 22 states in the US an attorney is required for closing. The remaining states will allow you to use a title company. In Ohio, all title companies have to either be owned by an attorney or the title company will be a part of the law firm.

Speaking with a few title companies our investors work with on a weekly basis, we have a few ideas, stories, and general practices to help not only title get your deals completed but also to help make those transactions smooth.

A great title company knows the ins and outs of real estate and what can be done and what cannot be done. For example, we worked on an assignment from one LLC to another LLC and we were a part of both LLC's. This did not work for us in these instances, but I do know a few mentors who have done it and come out of pocket with minimal, or receive funds back at closing. This is not a common practice and takes great patience and understanding so the next two people we will discuss in your team will be able to guide you in doing something like this.

SOMEONE IS AHEAD OF YOU, SEEK COUNSEL

A mentor is someone who is ahead of you in real estate that can help get you to your goals. There are mentors for every aspect of the real estate industry. Of the many qualities that a mentor should have there are a few we want to touch on.

Patience is a key thing for a mentor to have when dealing with a mentee. A mentor can be a great person and lack patience, which will make you not want to work with them. Patience is HUGE. There will be times where you don't understand something that has been said multiple times, but a mentor needs to know, understand, and assist you in learning. Patience is also good for when a deal falls through and your mentor doesn't understand how you made that decision but gives you grace and allows you to let it go.

Secondly, listening skills are a good thing to have. They can have patience but not listen and still be a bad mentor. A good mentor will listen and respond back to you what they believe to be your problem and then be able to help resolve it. If they do not understand the problem, they cannot help resolve it. For example, I was working with a guy that had issues with coming up with a downpayment on a triplex. The triplex numbers look good on paper. We discussed it a few days prior and he had his money coming from another source. That source fell through. Instead of discussing it with me, he pushed the deal back a few more days so he could get the cash. He and I already discussed working out a deal where I would front the money, and he would just pay me back when the funds were received. Since he pushed the deal back 2 days, that cost him another $250 out of pocket at closing. After I asked him why he pushed the deal back, I was also the buying agent for the deal, he advised he didn't have the funds at that time and needed to think of something to do. I talked him through a few things, and he got his funds within a few days and was able to close.

Lastly, from what I am going to talk about when looking for a mentor, empathy. A good mentor needs to be empathetic for their mentee. There are times when a mentee is down on their luck, or just wants to quit, a good mentor needs to recognize that and be able to step in to bridge the gap. They need to be able to show, with details, the best route to take and be able to guide you to next steps. The mentor needs to show you that you are capable of succeeding and help you navigate any problems that arise. A good mentor will also help you with problems you are facing as most times they will have faced similar problems and what they did to resolve the problems.

CPA

Certified Public Accountants (CPA) are amazing when it comes to having one on your team. From write offs, to tax strategies, exit strategies, and so on. In order to find the best one for you, there are a few things that you need to look for in a CPA. Before we got our CPA we were using an online tax company (before we really got into Real Estate Investing.) Our first year we went through an online tax service, and we were showing we owed the government $12,000. We were shocked and stunned and thought we would have to sell a property just to pay the taxes. We knew there were write offs but we didn't know what or how to do it. We reached out to a CPA that we have known for a while to take a look and give us guidance. He looked everything over and we actually got back $8,000 that year from taxes. We definitely were okay with paying him the $350 he charged us that year.

Here is a quick list of things to look for when finding an excellent CPA for your team. First, a great CPA should have longevity. They should not be right out of college and have all the time in the world to devote to you. A CPA that is hard to get a hold of, not impossible, schedules time for you to meet with them, and is ready to ask you questions on what you want out of real estate investing, is a great start. Longevity is key though. They need to know new laws that came out but also laws that have been in the books for a while.

My current CPA has been in the game for 25yrs. He is one of a multitude in his office with 20+yrs experience.

Secondly, a great CPA should provide tax strategies. Do you need to show a profit? Do you need to pay yourself out of your LLC? How much should you pay yourself? What is something you can write off? A great CPA will be able to assist you with all of these answers and more.

With how we have everything set up with our CPA, we file at the beginning of the year, and we send him the paperwork all in one. He reviews, calls me to set up an hour in person meeting where we go over all the questions he has for me, then he has it ready within another week or two. We have been with the same CPA's since and are very excited to see them making more money as we send them more people.

With all of your team, if they are not making you money, you need to find one that will. Whether it's a title company, mentor, CPA, lawyer, contractor, real estate agent or Property Manager. They may not have all the answers to every situation, but they should at least be making you money. It may be in the form of saving you money, like my CPA did. It may be in the form of not costing you more money down the road, as my contractors do with doing the job right the first time. But in every aspect of your team, they must make you money for it to be worth having them on the team.

CHAPTER 11

GETTING THE FIRST DEAL DONE

I believe everyone says this, but starting over there are things that I would do differently while investing in real estate. There are just so many things that you learn while going through the process and you realize what a boob you were in the beginning. If you've done a few deals, you can look back even now and think about the deals you would've done differently. I've spoken with many successful people in my days as a corporate employee. I listen to them and ask the one question, "Have you failed in business before?" With a resounding yes I would then follow up with, "Are you successful now because of what you learned in your failure?" I would instantly get another yes.

I'm not saying fail so that you will succeed, but when you do fail you will be able to get back on track faster than the first time you started. This is shown throughout many investors. No one wants to fail but should you fail, continue to grow and start over with your knowledge and get back to where you were before.

Julie and I bought our first investment property six months into our marriage. This was not a property that we failed on but there are plenty of things we learned along the way. Here are some of the details of our investment start up.

The property is a 4 bedroom, 1.5 bathroom, 2016 square foot two story brick home with an in-ground pool and a detached 2 car garage. We bought the property at the right time, 2012, where there were still plenty of foreclosures and not too many buyers. With that, we were able to get this property for $35,600. We had to put a roof on the sunroom the weekend after we closed. Over the course of the three years we lived there we put all new flooring in, painted, repaired the pool, and a new retaining wall and fence around the yard.

After three years we no longer wanted to be in town and wanted a property outside of city limits with land. We bought five acres of land for $22,000 in a great school district. We were set to look at building our next home. The property was a flagpole property with a house and another 1.3 acres that squared the property off. When we went to talk with the owners, our neighbors, they were ready for us and asked us, "So you're here to buy our house." After some negotiations we went ahead and bought the house and extra acreage for $128,000.

Now we have two properties and need to sell one of them. The housing market in our area still wasn't the greatest. There were houses selling but nothing was selling at top dollar. We decided to go ahead and place the home for sale on social media. After a few potential buyers that didn't pan out we were convinced we needed to look at selling through an agent. Then we got a contact from a couple that had been looking for a new home and have been in theirs for seven years. They introduced us to a land contract. The property was for sale for $80,000. The sellers could not get a traditional loan through a bank, and we did not need the cash up front but saw the opportunity to carry the note. We worked it out with the buyer that they would put $2,000 down on the property (again, first home owned and didn't know much about financing, especially seller-financing.) We gave them a 4.2% interest rate. We did not want to keep the note for 20 years and figured they would want to get a better rate, and go into a 30 year note, so we wrote up the deal with them having to use our lending for at least 3 years. So, for 3 years they couldn't refinance and get out of our loan together. Between years 3 and 5, they could shop around for another loan and no changes in the current note with us. After year 5, their interest rate went to 6%. Still, not horrible, but worked for us, and we hoped they would have refinanced and we could use the cash to buy the next property. We are in year 6 now and they still love paying us the 6% interest rate and have 14 years left. There are some other details in the deal that were fun to throw in as well. We knew the roof was going to need to be replaced very soon after selling the house, so we gave them $5,000 towards a new roof when that time came. Ultimately, we adjusted and paid for the entire roof, but wanted to make sure the property was taken care of. We also set in place that we could not finance the house for more than the buyers had left on the note, and if we did not pay the property taxes when they were due, the buyer would be able to pay the taxes instead of us. Overall, this has been a win for us and the buyers, and that is what it is about.

There are plenty of things you can point out that we did wrong in our first deal. Our next deals were much better.

Our previous house, 3rd home in 8yrs, we bought at an auction. It was a salon on the bottom and an apartment on top. Buying the property at auction I had two other investors to beat out on buying the property. One guy and I went back and forth until I hit $15,000. After $15,000, he backed out and the second guy jumped in. He was my previous broker, and I was not about to let him take the property for cheap. After I hit $20,000, he backed out. We closed a month later, and we took the profits from our previous house, the one with 6.5 acres, and put the money into doing a complete overhaul. Now, we have $60,000 into the property and do a cash out refinance. The appraisal came back at $196,000. Talk about a win. We were just looking to get around the $110,000 mark so we could refinance and pull around $70,000 out. Now we have the capital to buy more properties.

We are still a ways away from where we would like to be, completely full time investing, but we are at a point where we no longer have to work and can pay all of our bills with the rentals we have in play.

CHAPTER 12

BENEFITS OF INVESTING

What are some easy benefits of investing in real estate? What are some ways this will help your life? This chapter is about reaching for the benefits and guiding you to fulfill those benefits. Write down a few things that you see as a benefit of investing. Write it on the side, or on the bottom, or in a separate scrap piece of paper. What are the benefits that you can see right now?

_____

_____

_____

_____

_____

_____

Stop your 9-5 in 5 years. Cash Flow is a huge takeaway. As you grow your portfolio, you can step away from your 9-5 more and more. That trip to Australia you wanted to take? Go take it. Do you live in Ohio, like myself, and want to spend January in Florida? We did in our 4th year investing. Want a second home on the beach, or in the mountains? Go buy one and spend half the year living there.

Along with the benefits of cash flow, you'll also be able to write more off through your CPA. I am not going to make suggestions on what to write off, but check with your accountant on what and how to write off things you like to do. In general, you can write off what you own, utilities at that property, and any other property related expenses.

Building Lasting Wealth. Along with you no longer having a 9-5, you can ensure your kids do not have to have a 9-5. Teaching them the steps, being their mentor, and guiding them on the path will help you grow wealth that last generations.

Just these past few years we saw something we haven't seen like it in a long time. Inflation. Inflation kills a lot of industries. Real estate prices just keep rising along with inflation, and in our area, higher than inflation has risen. Our rental properties have gone from $400/mo for a 1 bedroom to almost $700/mo. That's low even to some of our larger cities, but we are in a smaller town and our prices are lower to purchase. Our last 2 triplexes were $50,000 and $51,500. They will gross $2,000/mo when we get through rehab, etc.

There are more benefits to owning real estate but these are a few of the main ones. What are some that you came up with? I'd love to hear them. Email me at HouseItStart@gmail.com

CHAPTER 13

SLAYING THE GIANTS

Should you be looking for that first real estate deal, whether it's a rental, flip, or wholesale, come to Ohio. I would be honored to help you get the deal done and will help guide you each step of the process. I can be reached at 419-632-3983 or my email HouseItStart@gmail.com

Why are you still reading? Get out there and get things done. The deals will keep coming. The sellers will keep selling. Wholesalers will continue to bring you the next property. Your title company wants your business. Your CPA has you covered. Your mentor is going to be on you, pushing you to close that first deal. GET THE FIRST DEAL DONE. Do not over-analyze. Run your numbers, make the offer, close the deal. Until next time, good luck. Hope to hear a success story from you shortly on how you took out the first deal and are now slaying the giants.

SUPPORTING YOUR VISIONARY

A NOTE FROM ADAM'S WIFE

Is your partner a visionary like mine? Are you ready to slay giants together, or is all this talk overwhelming and scary? Let me just tell you, Adam has had big dreams for years. I've done my best to support him along the way, but man, there was that one plan about 5 years ago… Well, let me just tell you about it.

It was a normal day, Adam was doing his real estate thing, and I just got home from a long day of work. I was ready to cuddle with my husband and kids after a long day and avoid all of the housework and to do lists. I'll be honest, what I'm getting ready to share is a little blurry, because it happened so fast, but my world was getting ready to be turned upside down.

Adam and I were just jumping into the real estate investment world. His mentor had told him that flips and rentals were the way to make sure we'd be financially secure. We had started the process through the help of a family friend who was acting as a private investor. I did my best to contribute and helped paint and clean up the new house on weeknights and weekends.

I knew Adam wanted to expand, and we had tossed around the idea of selling our house to get out of debt and jump start the business. There was just one issue, I really liked our house. We had over 6 acres in the country and lived very comfortably. Downsizing was going to be a sacrifice, and I wasn't sure it was the way to go.

Then Adam rocked my world. "I bought a house at auction today. It was only 20k."

I remember playfully responding in disbelief, "Oh, did you, now?"

He proceeded to tell me his grand plan. I do not know if I heard most of it because I was processing. I gave myself a quiet pep talk, "You can do this, Julie. Home is where ya'll are together. This sacrifice will be better for you in the long run... right? "

I had been reading a book by Johanna Gains. She talked about her husband Chip doing similar stunts. I figured, they were successful and she made it work, so I could too.

I knew our family would think we were nuts, and they were definitely wondering if we lost our minds, but I knew I was done making money for other people. We had just finished a crazy time at work, and I was expecting a large bonus because our profitability was through the roof. My bonus was half of what I projected. The business owners reaped the benefits of my efforts, and chose not to share. It was another catalyst moment for me, as if Adam buying the auction house was not enough, right? I knew I wanted to have more control and directly reap the benefits of my efforts. If you want to change your life radically, you have to live radically. Einstein said, Insanity is doing the same thing over and over again and expecting different results.

Knowing what I know now, I would give you the same pep talk. The sacrifices that need to be made to set yourself up for the future are worth it. Home is where ya'll are together. Be united and work alongside your partner.

The sacrifices were temporary and well worth it. I do not have to work. I work when I want to, but it is not required of me. I was the director of a call center working 60-80 hours a week, missing valuable time with my young kids. I resigned and followed my dreams to focus on our family. I've done business consulting work and homeschooled our kids. We traveled 13 weeks last year and over 8 weeks already this year. We have been able to volunteer our time and talents to help our local church and community. We even recently bought a home in my dream target area.

Sounds like a dream right? Well let me just tell you, I actually struggled to commit to buying the new house because of all of the sweet memories we had at our 20k auction house. Why, because the financial freedom we've gained along the way, allowed us to be stronger as a family and offered us more freedom that we could have imagined. That is what I value the most. The freedom to be a mom, wife, and business woman is such a blessing. There have been and will be struggles along the way, but it's worth it.

Do your research, pray about it, and go slay giants with your partner.

Julie Thornton